I SPY STARS

by Jenna Lee Gleis

TABLE OF CONTENTS

Words to Know 2

Star 3

Let's Review! 14

Answer Key 16

Index 16

 **Can you find the stars in this book?**
Flip to page 16 after reading to find out!

WORDS TO KNOW

big

fuzzy

points

red

shiny

star

STAR

point · · · ▶

A star has five points.

I spy a star!

5

Find the big star.

Find the red star.

Find the shiny star.

11

Find the fuzzy star.

LET'S REVIEW!

There are six stars in the image below. Can you find them?

ANSWER KEY

INDEX

big 7

fuzzy 13

points 3

red 9

shiny 11

star 3, 5, 7, 9, 11, 13